50 Cooking with Love Recipes

By: Kelly Johnson

Table of Contents

- Heart-shaped Pancakes
- Roasted Garlic Mashed Potatoes
- Classic Beef Stew
- Homemade Chicken Pot Pie
- Creamy Tomato Basil Soup
- Sweetheart Pasta with Garlic Butter Sauce
- Lobster Tail with Lemon Herb Butter
- Baked Salmon with Dill Sauce
- Chicken Alfredo Bake
- Shrimp and Grits
- Beef Tenderloin with Red Wine Sauce
- Chocolate-Covered Strawberries
- Lemon Blueberry Muffins
- Red Velvet Cupcakes with Cream Cheese Frosting
- Homemade Focaccia Bread
- Caramelized Onion and Brie Tart
- Roasted Vegetable Risotto

- Slow-Cooked Pulled Pork

- Panko-Crusted Chicken Tenders

- Grilled Veggie Skewers

- Chocolate Hazelnut Truffles

- Fresh Fruit Salad with Honey-Lime Dressing

- Classic Meatballs in Marinara Sauce

- Baked Macaroni and Cheese

- Buttery Garlic Shrimp

- Chocolate Cake with Ganache Frosting

- Spaghetti Carbonara

- Sweet Potato Casserole

- Warm Apple Crisp with Vanilla Ice Cream

- Crispy Chicken Parmesan

- Grilled Cheese and Tomato Soup

- Soft Pretzels with Mustard

- Mini Chicken and Waffle Bites

- Strawberry Shortcake with Whipped Cream

- Parmesan-Crusted Tilapia

- Braised Lamb Shanks

- Baked Ziti with Ricotta and Mozzarella
- Peach Cobbler with Cinnamon Streusel
- Chicken Piccata with Lemon Caper Sauce
- Stuffed Bell Peppers with Quinoa
- Homemade Chocolate Chip Cookies
- Raspberry Almond Bars
- Rosemary and Lemon Roasted Chicken
- Beef and Broccoli Stir-Fry
- Grilled Steak with Chimichurri Sauce
- Sweet Potato Fries with Sriracha Mayo
- White Chocolate Raspberry Cheesecake
- Lemon Poppy Seed Chicken Salad
- Warm Cinnamon Rolls
- Fettuccine Alfredo with Garlic Bread

Heart-shaped Pancakes

Ingredients:

- 1 1/2 cups all-purpose flour
- 3 1/2 tsp baking powder
- 1 tsp sugar
- 1/2 tsp salt
- 1 1/4 cups milk
- 1 egg
- 2 tbsp melted butter
- 1 tsp vanilla extract
- Butter or oil for cooking
- Maple syrup, whipped cream, and berries for serving

Instructions:

1. Preheat a griddle or non-stick pan over medium heat and lightly grease with butter or oil.
2. In a bowl, whisk together flour, baking powder, sugar, and salt.
3. In another bowl, combine milk, egg, melted butter, and vanilla extract.
4. Pour the wet ingredients into the dry ingredients and stir until just combined (don't overmix).
5. Using a heart-shaped cookie cutter (or a squeeze bottle), pour pancake batter onto the griddle in the shape of hearts.

6. Cook for about 2-3 minutes on each side, until golden brown.

7. Serve with maple syrup, whipped cream, and berries for a sweet touch.

Roasted Garlic Mashed Potatoes

Ingredients:

- 2 lbs potatoes, peeled and cut into chunks
- 1 head garlic, peeled and cloves separated
- 1/2 cup heavy cream
- 4 tbsp butter
- Salt and pepper to taste
- Fresh chives for garnish (optional)

Instructions:

1. Preheat the oven to 400°F (200°C). Wrap the garlic cloves in foil and roast for 20-25 minutes, until soft.
2. Meanwhile, boil the potatoes in a large pot of salted water until tender, about 15 minutes. Drain well.
3. In a small saucepan, heat the butter and cream over low heat until the butter is melted.
4. Squeeze the roasted garlic cloves into a bowl and mash them with a fork.
5. Mash the potatoes with a potato masher, adding the garlic mixture, salt, and pepper.
6. Continue mashing until smooth and creamy. Garnish with fresh chives if desired.

Classic Beef Stew

Ingredients:

- 1 1/2 lbs beef stew meat, cubed
- 1/4 cup all-purpose flour
- 3 tbsp vegetable oil
- 4 cups beef broth
- 1 onion, chopped
- 3 carrots, peeled and chopped
- 3 potatoes, peeled and chopped
- 2 cloves garlic, minced
- 1 tsp dried thyme
- 1 bay leaf
- Salt and pepper to taste

Instructions:

1. Toss the beef cubes in flour until evenly coated.
2. Heat oil in a large pot over medium-high heat. Brown the beef in batches, then set aside.
3. In the same pot, sauté the onion, garlic, and carrots until the onion is soft.
4. Add the browned beef back to the pot along with potatoes, beef broth, thyme, bay leaf, salt, and pepper.

5. Bring to a boil, then reduce heat and simmer for 1 1/2 to 2 hours, until the beef is tender and the stew has thickened.

6. Remove the bay leaf and serve hot.

Homemade Chicken Pot Pie

Ingredients:

- 1 lb cooked chicken, diced
- 2 cups frozen mixed vegetables
- 1/4 cup butter
- 1/4 cup all-purpose flour
- 2 cups chicken broth
- 1 cup heavy cream
- 1 tsp dried thyme
- Salt and pepper to taste
- 1 package refrigerated pie crusts (or homemade)

Instructions:

1. Preheat the oven to 400°F (200°C).
2. In a large saucepan, melt butter over medium heat. Stir in flour and cook for 1-2 minutes.
3. Gradually add chicken broth and heavy cream, stirring constantly until thickened, about 5 minutes.
4. Add the cooked chicken, mixed vegetables, thyme, salt, and pepper. Stir to combine.
5. Roll out one pie crust and fit it into a pie dish. Pour the chicken mixture into the crust.

6. Cover with the second pie crust and seal the edges. Cut small slits in the top for ventilation.

7. Bake for 30-35 minutes, or until golden brown and bubbly.

Creamy Tomato Basil Soup

Ingredients:

- 2 tbsp olive oil
- 1 onion, chopped
- 2 cloves garlic, minced
- 2 cans (14.5 oz each) diced tomatoes
- 1 cup chicken broth
- 1/2 cup heavy cream
- 1 tsp dried basil
- Salt and pepper to taste
- Fresh basil for garnish

Instructions:

1. Heat olive oil in a large pot over medium heat. Add the onion and garlic and cook until softened, about 5 minutes.
2. Add the diced tomatoes, chicken broth, basil, salt, and pepper. Bring to a simmer and cook for 15 minutes.
3. Use an immersion blender or regular blender to puree the soup until smooth.
4. Stir in the heavy cream and simmer for another 5 minutes.
5. Garnish with fresh basil before serving.

Sweetheart Pasta with Garlic Butter Sauce

Ingredients:

- 8 oz pasta (your choice, such as spaghetti or fettuccine)
- 4 tbsp butter
- 4 cloves garlic, minced
- 1/2 cup Parmesan cheese, grated
- Salt and pepper to taste
- Fresh parsley for garnish

Instructions:

1. Cook the pasta according to package instructions. Drain and set aside.
2. In a large skillet, melt butter over medium heat. Add the garlic and cook for 1-2 minutes, until fragrant.
3. Toss the cooked pasta in the garlic butter sauce, adding Parmesan cheese, salt, and pepper to taste.
4. Serve hot, garnished with fresh parsley.

Lobster Tail with Lemon Herb Butter

Ingredients:

- 2 lobster tails
- 4 tbsp butter, melted
- 1 clove garlic, minced
- 1 tbsp fresh lemon juice
- 1 tbsp fresh parsley, chopped
- Salt and pepper to taste

Instructions:

1. Preheat the oven to 425°F (220°C).
2. Using kitchen shears, cut the top of the lobster shell lengthwise. Gently pull the meat out and lay it on top of the shell.
3. In a small bowl, mix melted butter, garlic, lemon juice, parsley, salt, and pepper.
4. Brush the lobster meat with the lemon herb butter.
5. Place the lobster tails on a baking sheet and bake for 12-15 minutes, until the meat is opaque and tender.
6. Serve with extra lemon herb butter.

Baked Salmon with Dill Sauce

Ingredients:

- 4 salmon fillets
- 1 tbsp olive oil
- Salt and pepper to taste
- 1/2 cup sour cream
- 2 tbsp fresh dill, chopped
- 1 tbsp lemon juice
- 1 tsp Dijon mustard

Instructions:

1. Preheat the oven to 400°F (200°C). Line a baking sheet with parchment paper.
2. Rub the salmon fillets with olive oil, salt, and pepper. Place them on the baking sheet.
3. Bake for 12-15 minutes, or until the salmon is cooked through and flakes easily.
4. While the salmon bakes, mix sour cream, dill, lemon juice, and Dijon mustard in a small bowl.
5. Serve the salmon with a dollop of dill sauce on top.

Chicken Alfredo Bake

Ingredients:

- 2 cups cooked chicken, diced
- 12 oz pasta (penne or rotini works well)
- 2 cups Alfredo sauce (store-bought or homemade)
- 1 cup shredded mozzarella cheese
- 1/2 cup grated Parmesan cheese
- 1/4 tsp garlic powder
- Salt and pepper to taste

Instructions:

1. Preheat the oven to 375°F (190°C). Grease a baking dish.
2. Cook the pasta according to package instructions, then drain.
3. In a bowl, mix the cooked chicken, pasta, Alfredo sauce, mozzarella cheese, Parmesan cheese, garlic powder, salt, and pepper.
4. Pour the mixture into the prepared baking dish and bake for 20-25 minutes, until bubbly and golden on top.
5. Serve immediately.

Shrimp and Grits

Ingredients:

- 1 lb shrimp, peeled and deveined
- 1 cup grits (stone-ground preferred)
- 4 cups chicken broth
- 1/2 cup heavy cream
- 4 tbsp butter
- 2 cloves garlic, minced
- 1 tbsp lemon juice
- 1/4 tsp paprika
- Salt and pepper to taste
- Green onions for garnish

Instructions:

1. In a pot, bring chicken broth to a boil. Stir in the grits and reduce to a simmer. Cook according to package instructions until thick and creamy.
2. Stir in the heavy cream and butter. Season with salt and pepper.
3. In a separate skillet, melt butter over medium heat. Add garlic and cook until fragrant, about 1 minute.
4. Add shrimp, paprika, salt, and pepper. Cook until the shrimp are pink and cooked through, about 4-5 minutes.

5. Stir in lemon juice and serve the shrimp over the creamy grits. Garnish with green onions.

Beef Tenderloin with Red Wine Sauce

Ingredients:

- 1 beef tenderloin (about 2 lbs)
- 2 tbsp olive oil
- Salt and pepper to taste
- 1 tbsp butter
- 1 small onion, chopped
- 2 cloves garlic, minced
- 1 cup red wine (preferably dry)
- 1 cup beef broth
- 1 tbsp fresh thyme leaves
- 1 tbsp fresh rosemary, chopped

Instructions:

1. Preheat oven to 400°F (200°C). Season the beef tenderloin with salt and pepper.

2. Heat olive oil in a large oven-safe skillet over medium-high heat. Sear the tenderloin on all sides for about 2-3 minutes per side.

3. Transfer the skillet to the oven and roast for 20-25 minutes, or until the internal temperature reaches 130°F for medium-rare (or adjust to your preference).

4. Remove the beef from the oven and let it rest while you prepare the sauce.

5. In the same skillet, melt butter over medium heat. Add the onion and garlic and sauté until softened, about 3-4 minutes.

6. Add the red wine, beef broth, thyme, and rosemary. Bring to a simmer and cook for 10-15 minutes, until the sauce has reduced by half.

7. Slice the beef tenderloin and drizzle with the red wine sauce. Serve.

Chocolate-Covered Strawberries

Ingredients:

- 1 lb fresh strawberries, washed and dried
- 8 oz dark chocolate (or milk chocolate), chopped
- 4 oz white chocolate, chopped (optional, for drizzling)

Instructions:

1. Line a baking sheet with parchment paper.
2. Melt the dark chocolate in a heatproof bowl over a pot of simmering water (double boiler method) or microwave in 30-second intervals until smooth.
3. Dip each strawberry into the melted dark chocolate, coating it up to the green stem. Place it on the prepared baking sheet.
4. Melt the white chocolate (if using) and drizzle it over the dipped strawberries for a decorative touch.
5. Let the chocolate set at room temperature or refrigerate for 30 minutes until firm.

Lemon Blueberry Muffins

Ingredients:

- 1 1/2 cups all-purpose flour
- 1/2 cup sugar
- 2 tsp baking powder
- 1/2 tsp baking soda
- 1/4 tsp salt
- 1/2 cup milk
- 1/4 cup vegetable oil
- 1 large egg
- 1 tsp vanilla extract
- Zest of 1 lemon
- 1 tbsp fresh lemon juice
- 1 cup fresh blueberries (or frozen)
- 1 tbsp flour (for coating the blueberries)

Instructions:

1. Preheat oven to 375°F (190°C). Grease or line a muffin tin with paper liners.
2. In a bowl, whisk together flour, sugar, baking powder, baking soda, and salt.
3. In a separate bowl, mix together milk, vegetable oil, egg, vanilla extract, lemon zest, and lemon juice.

4. Pour the wet ingredients into the dry ingredients and stir until just combined.

5. Toss the blueberries in 1 tablespoon of flour, then fold them into the muffin batter.

6. Divide the batter evenly between the muffin cups.

7. Bake for 18-22 minutes, until a toothpick comes out clean. Let cool before serving.

Red Velvet Cupcakes with Cream Cheese Frosting

Ingredients:

- 1 1/2 cups all-purpose flour
- 1 cup sugar
- 1 tsp baking powder
- 1/2 tsp baking soda
- 1/2 tsp salt
- 1 tbsp cocoa powder
- 1/2 cup vegetable oil
- 1/2 cup buttermilk
- 1 large egg
- 1 tsp vanilla extract
- 1 tbsp red food coloring
- 1 tsp white vinegar
- 1/2 cup unsalted butter, softened
- 8 oz cream cheese, softened
- 4 cups powdered sugar
- 1 tsp vanilla extract

Instructions:

1. Preheat the oven to 350°F (175°C). Line a muffin tin with paper liners.

2. In a bowl, whisk together flour, sugar, baking powder, baking soda, salt, and cocoa powder.

3. In another bowl, mix together oil, buttermilk, egg, vanilla extract, food coloring, and vinegar.

4. Combine the wet and dry ingredients and stir until smooth.

5. Divide the batter evenly between the muffin cups.

6. Bake for 18-22 minutes, until a toothpick comes out clean. Let cool completely.

7. For the frosting, beat butter and cream cheese together until smooth. Gradually add powdered sugar and vanilla, and continue to beat until fluffy.

8. Frost the cooled cupcakes with the cream cheese frosting and enjoy.

Homemade Focaccia Bread

Ingredients:

- 2 1/4 tsp active dry yeast
- 1 1/2 cups warm water
- 1 tbsp sugar
- 3 1/2 cups all-purpose flour
- 2 tsp salt
- 1/4 cup olive oil, plus extra for drizzling
- 1 tsp dried rosemary (optional)
- Coarse sea salt for topping

Instructions:

1. In a bowl, dissolve yeast and sugar in warm water. Let it sit for 5 minutes until bubbly.
2. In a large bowl, combine flour and salt. Add the yeast mixture and 1/4 cup olive oil, stirring until a dough forms.
3. Knead the dough on a floured surface for 5-7 minutes, until smooth. Place the dough in a greased bowl, cover, and let it rise for 1-2 hours.
4. Preheat oven to 400°F (200°C). Punch the dough down and transfer it to a greased baking sheet. Stretch the dough to fit the pan.
5. Drizzle olive oil over the dough and sprinkle with rosemary and sea salt.
6. Bake for 20-25 minutes, until golden brown. Let cool slightly before slicing.

Caramelized Onion and Brie Tart

Ingredients:

- 1 sheet puff pastry, thawed
- 2 large onions, thinly sliced
- 2 tbsp butter
- 1 tbsp olive oil
- 1/2 tsp sugar
- 1/2 tsp salt
- 1/2 tsp black pepper
- 6 oz brie cheese, sliced
- Fresh thyme for garnish (optional)

Instructions:

1. Preheat oven to 375°F (190°C).
2. In a skillet, heat butter and olive oil over medium heat. Add the onions, sugar, salt, and pepper. Cook, stirring occasionally, for 25-30 minutes until the onions are deeply caramelized.
3. Roll out the puff pastry on a baking sheet. Spread the caramelized onions evenly over the pastry, leaving a small border around the edges.
4. Layer brie cheese slices on top of the onions.
5. Bake for 20-25 minutes, until the pastry is golden and puffed.
6. Garnish with fresh thyme before serving.

Roasted Vegetable Risotto

Ingredients:

- 1 cup Arborio rice
- 1 tbsp olive oil
- 1 small onion, chopped
- 2 cloves garlic, minced
- 1/2 cup white wine
- 4 cups vegetable broth, kept warm
- 1 cup roasted vegetables (carrots, zucchini, bell peppers, etc.)
- 1/4 cup grated Parmesan cheese
- Salt and pepper to taste

Instructions:

1. In a large skillet, heat olive oil over medium heat. Add the onion and garlic and cook until softened.
2. Stir in the rice and cook for 1-2 minutes, until lightly toasted.
3. Add the white wine and cook until absorbed.
4. Gradually add the warm vegetable broth, one ladle at a time, stirring constantly and allowing the liquid to be absorbed before adding more.
5. Continue this process until the rice is tender and creamy, about 18-20 minutes.
6. Stir in the roasted vegetables, Parmesan cheese, salt, and pepper. Serve hot.

Slow-Cooked Pulled Pork

Ingredients:

- 4 lb pork shoulder
- 1 onion, chopped
- 2 cloves garlic, minced
- 1 cup apple cider vinegar
- 1 cup chicken broth
- 2 tbsp brown sugar
- 1 tbsp paprika
- 1 tsp salt
- 1/2 tsp black pepper
- 1/2 tsp cumin
- 1/2 tsp chili powder

Instructions:

1. In a slow cooker, combine onion, garlic, apple cider vinegar, chicken broth, brown sugar, paprika, salt, pepper, cumin, and chili powder.
2. Place the pork shoulder in the slow cooker and coat it with the seasoning mixture.
3. Cover and cook on low for 8-10 hours, until the pork is tender and shreds easily.
4. Shred the pork with two forks and mix it with the juices from the slow cooker. Serve with buns or on its own.

Panko-Crusted Chicken Tenders

Ingredients:

- 1 lb chicken breast tenders
- 1 cup panko breadcrumbs
- 1/2 cup all-purpose flour
- 2 eggs, beaten
- 1/2 tsp garlic powder
- 1/2 tsp paprika
- Salt and pepper to taste
- Vegetable oil for frying

Instructions:

1. In a shallow bowl, mix together panko breadcrumbs, garlic powder, paprika, salt, and pepper.
2. In another shallow bowl, place the flour, and in a third bowl, place the beaten eggs.
3. Dredge the chicken tenders first in the flour, then dip in the egg, and finally coat in the panko mixture.
4. Heat oil in a large skillet over medium heat. Fry the chicken tenders for 3-4 minutes per side, until golden brown and cooked through.
5. Serve hot with dipping sauce.

Grilled Veggie Skewers

Ingredients:

- 1 zucchini, sliced
- 1 red bell pepper, cut into chunks
- 1 yellow bell pepper, cut into chunks
- 1 red onion, cut into chunks
- 1 pint cherry tomatoes
- 1 cup mushrooms, whole or halved
- 2 tbsp olive oil
- 1 tbsp balsamic vinegar
- 1 tsp garlic powder
- 1 tsp dried oregano
- Salt and pepper to taste
- Wooden skewers (soaked in water for 30 minutes)

Instructions:

1. Preheat the grill to medium-high heat.
2. In a large bowl, toss the veggies with olive oil, balsamic vinegar, garlic powder, oregano, salt, and pepper.
3. Thread the vegetables onto the soaked skewers, alternating them as desired.

4. Grill the skewers for 8-10 minutes, turning occasionally, until the veggies are tender and slightly charred.

5. Serve warm.

Chocolate Hazelnut Truffles

Ingredients:

- 8 oz dark chocolate (chopped)
- 1/2 cup heavy cream
- 2 tbsp unsalted butter
- 1/2 tsp vanilla extract
- 1/4 cup hazelnuts, chopped (for coating)

Instructions:

1. In a heatproof bowl, combine the chopped chocolate, heavy cream, and butter.
2. Place the bowl over a pot of simmering water (double boiler method) and stir until the chocolate is completely melted and smooth.
3. Remove from heat and stir in vanilla extract.
4. Let the mixture cool to room temperature, then refrigerate for 1-2 hours, or until firm enough to shape.
5. Scoop the chilled chocolate mixture into small balls and roll them in the chopped hazelnuts.
6. Refrigerate the truffles until firm. Serve cold or at room temperature.

Fresh Fruit Salad with Honey-Lime Dressing

Ingredients:

- 1 cup strawberries, sliced
- 1 cup blueberries
- 1 cup pineapple, diced
- 1 cup watermelon, diced
- 1 orange, peeled and segmented
- 1 kiwi, peeled and sliced
- 2 tbsp honey
- 1 tbsp lime juice
- 1/2 tsp lime zest

Instructions:

1. In a large bowl, combine all the fresh fruit.
2. In a small bowl, whisk together honey, lime juice, and lime zest.
3. Drizzle the honey-lime dressing over the fruit salad and gently toss to combine.
4. Serve chilled.

Classic Meatballs in Marinara Sauce

Ingredients:

- 1 lb ground beef
- 1/4 cup breadcrumbs
- 1/4 cup grated Parmesan cheese
- 1 large egg
- 2 cloves garlic, minced
- 1 tsp dried oregano
- Salt and pepper to taste
- 2 cups marinara sauce (store-bought or homemade)

Instructions:

1. Preheat the oven to 375°F (190°C). Line a baking sheet with parchment paper.
2. In a bowl, combine ground beef, breadcrumbs, Parmesan cheese, egg, garlic, oregano, salt, and pepper. Mix until fully combined.
3. Roll the mixture into meatballs, about 1 inch in diameter, and place them on the prepared baking sheet.
4. Bake for 20-25 minutes, or until the meatballs are browned and cooked through.
5. In a large saucepan, heat the marinara sauce over medium heat. Add the meatballs to the sauce and simmer for 10-15 minutes, allowing the flavors to meld.
6. Serve with pasta, on a sub roll, or on their own.

Baked Macaroni and Cheese

Ingredients:

- 1 lb elbow macaroni
- 2 cups shredded cheddar cheese
- 1 cup shredded mozzarella cheese
- 2 cups milk
- 1/4 cup unsalted butter
- 1/4 cup all-purpose flour
- 1/2 tsp garlic powder
- 1/2 tsp onion powder
- Salt and pepper to taste
- 1/2 cup breadcrumbs (optional for topping)

Instructions:

1. Preheat oven to 350°F (175°C). Grease a 9x13-inch baking dish.
2. Cook the macaroni according to package instructions, drain, and set aside.
3. In a saucepan, melt butter over medium heat. Stir in the flour and cook for 1-2 minutes, until golden.
4. Gradually whisk in the milk and cook, stirring constantly, until the sauce thickens.
5. Stir in the cheddar cheese, mozzarella cheese, garlic powder, onion powder, salt, and pepper. Continue to stir until the cheese is melted and smooth.

6. Combine the cheese sauce with the cooked macaroni, then transfer the mixture to the prepared baking dish.

7. Top with breadcrumbs (if desired) and bake for 20-25 minutes, until bubbly and golden.

8. Serve hot.

Buttery Garlic Shrimp

Ingredients:

- 1 lb large shrimp, peeled and deveined
- 3 tbsp unsalted butter
- 4 cloves garlic, minced
- 1/4 tsp red pepper flakes (optional)
- Salt and pepper to taste
- 2 tbsp fresh parsley, chopped
- 1 tbsp lemon juice

Instructions:

1. Heat butter in a large skillet over medium heat.
2. Add the garlic and red pepper flakes (if using) and sauté for 1-2 minutes until fragrant.
3. Add the shrimp to the skillet and season with salt and pepper. Cook for 2-3 minutes on each side, until the shrimp are pink and cooked through.
4. Remove from heat and drizzle with lemon juice. Sprinkle with fresh parsley.
5. Serve immediately with rice, pasta, or crusty bread.

Chocolate Cake with Ganache Frosting

Ingredients:

- 1 3/4 cups all-purpose flour
- 1 1/2 cups sugar
- 1/2 cup unsweetened cocoa powder
- 1 1/2 tsp baking powder
- 1 tsp baking soda
- 1/2 tsp salt
- 2 large eggs
- 1 cup buttermilk
- 1/2 cup vegetable oil
- 2 tsp vanilla extract
- 1 cup boiling water

For the Ganache:

- 8 oz dark chocolate, chopped
- 1 cup heavy cream

Instructions:

1. Preheat oven to 350°F (175°C). Grease and flour two 9-inch round cake pans.

2. In a large bowl, whisk together the flour, sugar, cocoa powder, baking powder, baking soda, and salt.

3. Add the eggs, buttermilk, oil, and vanilla extract. Mix until smooth.

4. Gradually add the boiling water and stir until the batter is thin and well combined.

5. Pour the batter into the prepared cake pans and bake for 30-35 minutes, or until a toothpick inserted into the center comes out clean.

6. While the cakes are cooling, prepare the ganache. Heat the heavy cream in a saucepan until it just begins to simmer. Pour the cream over the chopped chocolate and stir until smooth and glossy.

7. Once the cakes have cooled, spread the ganache over the top of one layer, place the second layer on top, and frost the entire cake.

8. Serve and enjoy!

Spaghetti Carbonara

Ingredients:

- 1 lb spaghetti
- 4 oz pancetta or bacon, diced
- 2 large eggs
- 1 cup grated Parmesan cheese
- 1/2 tsp black pepper
- Salt to taste
- 2 cloves garlic, minced
- 2 tbsp olive oil

Instructions:

1. Cook the spaghetti according to package instructions. Reserve 1/2 cup of pasta water before draining.

2. In a large skillet, heat olive oil over medium heat. Add the pancetta or bacon and cook until crispy.

3. Add garlic to the skillet and cook for another 1-2 minutes.

4. In a bowl, whisk together eggs, Parmesan cheese, black pepper, and salt.

5. Add the drained pasta to the skillet and toss to coat in the pancetta and garlic mixture.

6. Remove the skillet from the heat and quickly stir in the egg mixture, adding reserved pasta water as needed to create a creamy sauce.

7. Serve immediately with extra Parmesan cheese and black pepper.

Sweet Potato Casserole

Ingredients:

- 4 medium sweet potatoes, peeled and cubed
- 1/4 cup brown sugar
- 1/4 cup melted butter
- 1/2 tsp vanilla extract
- 1/4 tsp cinnamon
- 1/4 tsp nutmeg
- 1/4 cup milk
- 1/2 cup mini marshmallows (optional)

Instructions:

1. Preheat oven to 350°F (175°C). Grease a baking dish.
2. Boil sweet potatoes in a pot of water for 10-15 minutes, or until tender. Drain and mash.
3. In a bowl, combine the mashed sweet potatoes, brown sugar, melted butter, vanilla extract, cinnamon, nutmeg, and milk.
4. Transfer the mixture to the prepared baking dish and smooth the top.
5. If desired, top with mini marshmallows and bake for 20 minutes, or until golden and bubbly.
6. Serve warm.

Warm Apple Crisp with Vanilla Ice Cream

Ingredients:

- 6 apples, peeled, cored, and sliced
- 1/4 cup sugar
- 1 tsp cinnamon
- 1/2 cup oats
- 1/2 cup flour
- 1/4 cup brown sugar
- 1/4 cup unsalted butter, cubed
- Vanilla ice cream for serving

Instructions:

1. Preheat oven to 350°F (175°C). Grease a baking dish.
2. Toss the apple slices with sugar and cinnamon, then place in the prepared dish.
3. In a bowl, combine oats, flour, brown sugar, and cubed butter. Use a pastry cutter or your hands to mix until the mixture resembles coarse crumbs.
4. Sprinkle the topping evenly over the apples.
5. Bake for 40-45 minutes, until the topping is golden brown and the apples are tender.
6. Serve warm with vanilla ice cream.

Crispy Chicken Parmesan

Ingredients:

- 4 boneless, skinless chicken breasts
- 1 cup all-purpose flour
- 2 large eggs, beaten
- 2 cups breadcrumbs (preferably Panko)
- 1 cup grated Parmesan cheese
- 2 cups marinara sauce
- 1 1/2 cups mozzarella cheese, shredded
- Olive oil for frying
- Fresh basil for garnish (optional)

Instructions:

1. Preheat oven to 375°F (190°C). Grease a baking dish.
2. Dredge the chicken breasts in flour, then dip into the beaten eggs, and coat with breadcrumbs and Parmesan cheese.
3. Heat olive oil in a skillet over medium heat. Fry the chicken for 4-5 minutes per side, until golden brown and crispy.
4. Transfer the chicken breasts to the prepared baking dish and top with marinara sauce and shredded mozzarella.
5. Bake for 20 minutes, until the cheese is melted and bubbly.
6. Garnish with fresh basil before serving.

Grilled Cheese and Tomato Soup

Ingredients for Grilled Cheese:

- 8 slices of bread (your choice)
- 4 tbsp butter
- 8 slices of cheddar cheese

Ingredients for Tomato Soup:

- 1 can (28 oz) crushed tomatoes
- 1 cup vegetable broth
- 1/2 cup heavy cream
- 1/2 onion, chopped
- 2 cloves garlic, minced
- 1 tbsp olive oil
- 1 tsp dried basil
- Salt and pepper to taste

Instructions:

1. **For the Soup:**
    - Heat olive oil in a pot over medium heat. Add the onion and garlic, cooking until softened (about 5 minutes).
    - Add the crushed tomatoes, vegetable broth, basil, salt, and pepper. Bring to a boil.

- Reduce heat and simmer for 15-20 minutes.
- Stir in the heavy cream and simmer for another 5 minutes. Use an immersion blender to smooth out the soup or leave it chunky, depending on preference.
- Keep warm.

2. **For the Grilled Cheese:**
   - Heat a skillet over medium heat.
   - Butter one side of each slice of bread. Place cheese slices between two slices of bread, buttered sides out.
   - Grill the sandwiches in the skillet, flipping once, until golden brown on both sides and the cheese is melted (about 4-5 minutes per side).

3. Serve the grilled cheese sandwiches with a bowl of tomato soup.

Soft Pretzels with Mustard

Ingredients:

- 2 1/4 tsp active dry yeast
- 1 1/2 cups warm water
- 4 cups all-purpose flour
- 1 tbsp sugar
- 1 tsp salt
- 2 tbsp melted butter
- 1/4 cup baking soda
- 1 large egg (for egg wash)
- Coarse sea salt
- Mustard for dipping

Instructions:

1. In a bowl, dissolve the yeast and sugar in warm water. Let sit for 5 minutes, or until foamy.
2. Add the flour, salt, and melted butter to the yeast mixture. Stir until combined, then knead for about 5-7 minutes until smooth.
3. Let the dough rise in a greased bowl, covered, for 1 hour, or until doubled in size.
4. Preheat oven to 450°F (230°C). Line a baking sheet with parchment paper.
5. Punch down the dough and divide it into 8 equal pieces. Roll each piece into a long rope and form into a pretzel shape.

6. Bring a large pot of water to a boil, add baking soda. Drop the pretzels one at a time into the boiling water for 30 seconds, then remove and place on the baking sheet.

7. Brush the pretzels with the egg wash and sprinkle with coarse sea salt.

8. Bake for 12-15 minutes or until golden brown. Serve with mustard for dipping.

Mini Chicken and Waffle Bites

Ingredients:

- 1 lb boneless, skinless chicken tenders
- 1/2 cup flour
- 1 tsp paprika
- 1/2 tsp salt
- 1/4 tsp black pepper
- 2 eggs, beaten
- 1 1/2 cups waffle mix (plus ingredients required for waffles)
- Maple syrup for drizzling

Instructions:

1. Preheat the oven to 400°F (200°C). Line a baking sheet with parchment paper.
2. In a shallow bowl, mix flour, paprika, salt, and pepper.
3. Dredge the chicken tenders in the flour mixture, then dip into beaten eggs.
4. Cook the chicken tenders in a hot skillet with oil for 3-4 minutes on each side, or until golden brown and cooked through.
5. Prepare mini waffles using a waffle iron, following the instructions on the waffle mix package.
6. Once waffles are cooked, cut them into small bite-sized pieces.
7. Serve the chicken tenders on top of the mini waffles, drizzled with maple syrup.

Strawberry Shortcake with Whipped Cream

Ingredients:

- 1 lb strawberries, hulled and sliced
- 1/4 cup sugar (for strawberries)
- 2 cups heavy cream
- 2 tbsp powdered sugar
- 1 tsp vanilla extract
- 4 shortcake biscuits (store-bought or homemade)

Instructions:

1. Toss the sliced strawberries with 1/4 cup sugar and set aside to macerate for at least 30 minutes.
2. In a chilled bowl, whip the heavy cream with powdered sugar and vanilla extract until soft peaks form.
3. Slice the shortcake biscuits in half. Layer the bottom half with macerated strawberries and a generous dollop of whipped cream. Top with the other half of the biscuit.
4. Serve immediately with extra whipped cream and strawberries on top.

Parmesan-Crusted Tilapia

Ingredients:

- 4 tilapia fillets
- 1/2 cup grated Parmesan cheese
- 1/4 cup breadcrumbs
- 1 tsp garlic powder
- Salt and pepper to taste
- 2 tbsp olive oil

Instructions:

1. Preheat the oven to 400°F (200°C). Line a baking sheet with parchment paper.
2. In a shallow dish, combine Parmesan cheese, breadcrumbs, garlic powder, salt, and pepper.
3. Coat the tilapia fillets with the breadcrumb mixture, pressing gently to adhere.
4. Heat olive oil in a skillet over medium heat. Cook the fillets for 2-3 minutes per side until golden brown.
5. Transfer the fillets to the baking sheet and bake for 10 minutes, or until the fish flakes easily with a fork.
6. Serve with lemon wedges and your favorite side dishes.

Braised Lamb Shanks

Ingredients:

- 4 lamb shanks
- 2 tbsp olive oil
- 1 onion, chopped
- 2 carrots, chopped
- 2 celery stalks, chopped
- 3 cloves garlic, minced
- 2 cups red wine
- 3 cups beef or vegetable broth
- 2 sprigs fresh rosemary
- Salt and pepper to taste

Instructions:

1. Preheat the oven to 325°F (163°C).

2. Heat olive oil in a large oven-safe pot over medium-high heat. Season the lamb shanks with salt and pepper and sear on all sides until browned (about 5-7 minutes).

3. Remove the lamb shanks and set aside. Add the chopped onion, carrots, celery, and garlic to the pot and sauté for 5 minutes.

4. Pour in the red wine and broth, scraping the bottom of the pot to release any browned bits. Add rosemary.

5. Return the lamb shanks to the pot and cover with a lid.

6. Braise in the oven for 2-3 hours, until the lamb is tender and falls off the bone.

7. Serve the lamb shanks with the braising liquid and vegetables.

Baked Ziti with Ricotta and Mozzarella

Ingredients:

- 1 lb ziti pasta
- 2 cups marinara sauce
- 1 1/2 cups ricotta cheese
- 1 1/2 cups shredded mozzarella cheese
- 1/2 cup grated Parmesan cheese
- 1 egg, beaten
- 2 tbsp fresh basil, chopped
- Salt and pepper to taste

Instructions:

1. Preheat the oven to 375°F (190°C). Grease a 9x13-inch baking dish.
2. Cook the ziti pasta according to package directions, drain, and set aside.
3. In a bowl, combine the ricotta cheese, 1 cup mozzarella cheese, Parmesan cheese, beaten egg, basil, salt, and pepper.
4. Toss the cooked pasta with marinara sauce, then fold in the cheese mixture.
5. Pour the pasta mixture into the baking dish and top with the remaining mozzarella cheese.
6. Bake for 25-30 minutes, or until bubbly and golden on top.

Peach Cobbler with Cinnamon Streusel

Ingredients for Cobbler:

- 4 cups fresh or canned peaches, drained
- 1/4 cup sugar
- 1 tsp vanilla extract
- 1 tbsp cornstarch

Ingredients for Streusel:

- 1/2 cup all-purpose flour
- 1/4 cup sugar
- 1/2 tsp cinnamon
- 1/4 cup unsalted butter, cold and cubed

Instructions:

1. Preheat the oven to 350°F (175°C). Grease a baking dish.
2. Toss the peaches with sugar, vanilla, and cornstarch. Place them in the prepared dish.
3. In a separate bowl, combine flour, sugar, and cinnamon. Cut in the cold butter until the mixture resembles coarse crumbs.
4. Sprinkle the streusel topping over the peaches.
5. Bake for 40-45 minutes, until the topping is golden and the fruit is bubbling.

Chicken Piccata with Lemon Caper Sauce

Ingredients:

- 4 boneless, skinless chicken breasts
- 1/2 cup flour
- 1/4 cup olive oil
- 1/4 cup fresh lemon juice
- 1/4 cup capers
- 1 cup chicken broth
- Salt and pepper to taste
- Fresh parsley for garnish

Instructions:

1. Season the chicken breasts with salt and pepper, then dredge in flour.
2. Heat olive oil in a skillet over medium-high heat. Cook the chicken breasts for 3-4 minutes per side until golden and cooked through.
3. Remove the chicken from the skillet and set aside.
4. In the same skillet, add chicken broth, lemon juice, and capers. Bring to a boil and cook for 2 minutes.
5. Return the chicken to the skillet and simmer for 3-4 minutes, allowing the sauce to reduce slightly.
6. Garnish with fresh parsley and serve with your favorite side.

Stuffed Bell Peppers with Quinoa

Ingredients:

- 4 bell peppers, tops cut off and seeds removed
- 1 cup cooked quinoa
- 1 can (15 oz) black beans, drained and rinsed
- 1 cup corn kernels
- 1/2 cup shredded cheese
- 1 tsp cumin
- 1 tsp chili powder
- Salt and pepper to taste

Instructions:

1. Preheat oven to 375°F (190°C). Grease a baking dish.
2. Mix quinoa, black beans, corn, cheese, cumin, chili powder, salt, and pepper in a bowl.
3. Stuff the bell peppers with the quinoa mixture.
4. Place the stuffed peppers in the baking dish and cover with foil.
5. Bake for 30 minutes, then remove the foil and bake for an additional 10 minutes, until the peppers are tender.

Homemade Chocolate Chip Cookies

Ingredients:

- 2 1/4 cups all-purpose flour
- 1 tsp baking soda
- 1/2 tsp salt
- 1 cup unsalted butter, softened
- 3/4 cup brown sugar
- 3/4 cup granulated sugar
- 2 large eggs
- 2 tsp vanilla extract
- 2 cups semisweet chocolate chips

Instructions:

1. Preheat oven to 350°F (175°C). Line a baking sheet with parchment paper.
2. In a bowl, combine flour, baking soda, and salt.
3. In a separate bowl, beat the butter with both sugars until creamy. Add eggs, one at a time, and vanilla.
4. Gradually add the flour mixture, mixing until just combined. Stir in chocolate chips.
5. Drop tablespoon-sized dough onto the baking sheet. Bake for 10-12 minutes, or until golden brown.
6. Let cool on a wire rack.

Raspberry Almond Bars

Ingredients:

- 1 cup all-purpose flour
- 1/2 cup almond meal
- 1/4 cup sugar
- 1/4 tsp salt
- 1/2 cup unsalted butter, softened
- 1 egg
- 1/2 tsp vanilla extract
- 1/2 cup raspberry jam
- 1/4 cup sliced almonds

Instructions:

1. Preheat the oven to 350°F (175°C). Grease a 9x9-inch baking pan.
2. Mix flour, almond meal, sugar, and salt in a bowl. Add butter and blend until crumbly.
3. Stir in the egg and vanilla extract. Press the dough into the prepared pan.
4. Spread raspberry jam over the dough and sprinkle with sliced almonds.
5. Bake for 25-30 minutes, or until golden. Let cool before cutting into bars.

Rosemary and Lemon Roasted Chicken

Ingredients:

- 1 whole chicken (about 4-5 lbs)
- 2 lemons, halved
- 3-4 sprigs fresh rosemary
- 4 cloves garlic, smashed
- 1/4 cup olive oil
- 1 tsp salt
- 1/2 tsp black pepper
- 1/2 cup white wine (optional)

Instructions:

1. Preheat the oven to 425°F (220°C). Pat the chicken dry with paper towels.
2. Rub the chicken inside and out with olive oil. Season with salt and pepper.
3. Stuff the cavity with lemon halves, rosemary sprigs, and garlic.
4. Place the chicken on a roasting rack in a roasting pan. Optionally, pour white wine around the chicken for added flavor and moisture.
5. Roast the chicken for 1 hour 15 minutes to 1 hour 30 minutes, or until the internal temperature reaches 165°F (74°C).
6. Let the chicken rest for 10-15 minutes before carving. Serve with roasted vegetables or your favorite side.

Beef and Broccoli Stir-Fry

Ingredients:

- 1 lb flank steak, thinly sliced against the grain
- 2 tbsp vegetable oil
- 1 tbsp garlic, minced
- 1 tbsp ginger, grated
- 2 cups broccoli florets
- 1/4 cup soy sauce
- 1 tbsp oyster sauce
- 1 tbsp hoisin sauce
- 1 tsp sesame oil
- 1 tsp cornstarch (optional for thickening)
- Cooked rice, for serving

Instructions:

1. Heat 1 tbsp vegetable oil in a large skillet or wok over medium-high heat.
2. Add the sliced beef and stir-fry for 2-3 minutes until browned. Remove and set aside.
3. In the same pan, add the remaining oil. Stir in garlic and ginger, cooking for 30 seconds.
4. Add the broccoli florets and stir-fry for 3-4 minutes until tender-crisp.

5. In a small bowl, mix the soy sauce, oyster sauce, hoisin sauce, sesame oil, and cornstarch (if using).

6. Add the beef back into the pan, pour the sauce over, and stir to coat. Cook for an additional 2 minutes.

7. Serve over cooked rice and garnish with sesame seeds or green onions.

Grilled Steak with Chimichurri Sauce

Ingredients for Steak:

- 2 ribeye steaks or your preferred cut (about 1 inch thick)
- Salt and pepper, to taste
- Olive oil for grilling

Ingredients for Chimichurri Sauce:

- 1/2 cup fresh parsley, finely chopped
- 2 tbsp fresh oregano, finely chopped (or 1 tbsp dried)
- 2 cloves garlic, minced
- 1/4 cup red wine vinegar
- 1/2 cup olive oil
- 1/2 tsp red pepper flakes (optional)
- Salt and pepper, to taste

Instructions:

1. Preheat your grill to medium-high heat.
2. Season the steaks with salt and pepper, and brush with olive oil.
3. Grill the steaks for about 4-5 minutes per side for medium-rare, or longer to your preferred doneness.
4. While the steaks are grilling, prepare the chimichurri sauce: Combine the parsley, oregano, garlic, vinegar, olive oil, red pepper flakes, salt, and pepper in a bowl. Mix

well.

5. Remove the steaks from the grill and let rest for 5 minutes.

6. Serve the steaks with chimichurri sauce on top or on the side.

Sweet Potato Fries with Sriracha Mayo

Ingredients for Fries:

- 2 large sweet potatoes, peeled and cut into fries
- 2 tbsp olive oil
- 1/2 tsp paprika
- 1/2 tsp garlic powder
- Salt and pepper, to taste

Ingredients for Sriracha Mayo:

- 1/2 cup mayonnaise
- 1 tbsp sriracha sauce (adjust to taste)
- 1 tsp lime juice
- Salt, to taste

Instructions:

1. Preheat the oven to 425°F (220°C). Line a baking sheet with parchment paper.
2. Toss the sweet potato fries with olive oil, paprika, garlic powder, salt, and pepper. Spread them out evenly on the baking sheet.
3. Bake for 25-30 minutes, flipping halfway through, until crispy and golden.
4. While the fries are baking, mix the mayonnaise, sriracha, lime juice, and a pinch of salt in a small bowl.
5. Serve the fries hot with the sriracha mayo for dipping.

White Chocolate Raspberry Cheesecake

Ingredients for Crust:

- 1 1/2 cups graham cracker crumbs
- 1/4 cup melted butter
- 1/4 cup sugar

Ingredients for Filling:

- 3 cups cream cheese, softened
- 1 cup sugar
- 2 cups white chocolate chips, melted
- 1 tsp vanilla extract
- 3 large eggs
- 1/2 cup sour cream
- 1/2 cup fresh raspberries (for swirl)

Instructions:

1. Preheat the oven to 325°F (165°C). Grease a 9-inch springform pan and line the bottom with parchment paper.

2. In a bowl, mix the graham cracker crumbs, melted butter, and sugar. Press into the bottom of the pan to form a crust.

3. In a separate bowl, beat the cream cheese and sugar until smooth. Add the melted white chocolate and vanilla extract, mixing until combined.

4. Add the eggs, one at a time, beating well after each addition. Stir in sour cream until smooth.

5. Pour the cheesecake batter into the prepared crust.

6. Drop spoonfuls of raspberries onto the batter and swirl gently with a knife.

7. Bake for 55-65 minutes, or until the center is set. Let the cheesecake cool, then refrigerate for at least 4 hours before serving.

Lemon Poppy Seed Chicken Salad

Ingredients:

- 2 chicken breasts, cooked and shredded
- 1/2 cup mayonnaise
- 2 tbsp Greek yogurt
- 1 tbsp lemon juice
- 1 tsp lemon zest
- 1 tbsp poppy seeds
- 1/4 cup celery, finely chopped
- Salt and pepper, to taste

Instructions:

1. In a large bowl, combine the mayonnaise, Greek yogurt, lemon juice, lemon zest, poppy seeds, celery, salt, and pepper.
2. Add the shredded chicken to the mixture and stir until well combined.
3. Serve as a sandwich, wrap, or over a bed of greens.

Warm Cinnamon Rolls

Ingredients for Dough:

- 3 cups all-purpose flour
- 1/4 cup sugar
- 1 packet active dry yeast
- 1/2 cup warm milk
- 1/4 cup melted butter
- 1/2 tsp salt
- 2 large eggs

Ingredients for Filling:

- 1/2 cup softened butter
- 1/2 cup brown sugar
- 2 tbsp ground cinnamon

Ingredients for Frosting:

- 1 cup powdered sugar
- 2 oz cream cheese, softened
- 1 tbsp milk
- 1/2 tsp vanilla extract

Instructions:

1. In a bowl, dissolve yeast in warm milk and let sit for 5 minutes. Add sugar, melted butter, eggs, and salt, mixing well.

2. Gradually add flour and knead until the dough is smooth. Cover and let rise for 1 hour.

3. Preheat the oven to 350°F (175°C). Roll the dough into a large rectangle.

4. Spread softened butter over the dough and sprinkle with brown sugar and cinnamon. Roll up the dough and cut into 12 slices.

5. Place the rolls in a greased pan and let rise for 30 minutes.

6. Bake for 25-30 minutes until golden.

7. Mix the frosting ingredients together and spread over the warm rolls.

Fettuccine Alfredo with Garlic Bread

Ingredients for Fettuccine Alfredo:

- 1 lb fettuccine pasta
- 1 cup heavy cream
- 1/2 cup butter
- 1 1/2 cups grated Parmesan cheese
- Salt and pepper, to taste
- Fresh parsley, chopped

Ingredients for Garlic Bread:

- 1 loaf French bread
- 1/2 cup unsalted butter, softened
- 3 cloves garlic, minced
- 1 tbsp fresh parsley, chopped

Instructions for Alfredo:

1. Cook the fettuccine according to package directions. Drain and set aside.
2. In a large pan, melt butter over medium heat. Add the cream and bring to a simmer.
3. Stir in Parmesan cheese, salt, and pepper. Cook for 2-3 minutes until the sauce thickens.
4. Toss the fettuccine in the sauce, then sprinkle with fresh parsley.

Instructions for Garlic Bread:

1. Preheat the oven to 375°F (190°C).

2. Slice the French bread in half lengthwise. Mix butter, garlic, and parsley in a bowl and spread over the bread.

3. Bake for 10-12 minutes until golden brown. Slice and serve with the fettuccine Alfredo.